Printed in the United States of America

First Printing, 2021

https://www.coachingwithdramandamorris.com

Dedicated to those pioneers who had the intuition and confidence to recognize the Earth as medicine.
Who dared speak on topics not yet recognized or accepted by the mainstream culture.
To those who have translated this intuition through extensive modern discovery and research.
And to my dear readers, who are willing to incorporate earthing as part of your child's well-being.

I appreciate all of you.

Dirty Toes

A Child's Guide to Earthing

Amanda Morris PsyD
Illustrated by Winda Lee

Dear Reader,

When we walk barefoot on the dirt, sit on the ground for a picnic, or lay on the grass for a nap, we are doing something called earthing or grounding. These words are interchangeable.

Being grounded has two different meanings.

1. When you are in trouble and your parents take away your favorite things.
2. Being physically connected to the surface of the Earth.

In this book we are going to read about number 2. Being physically connected to the surface of the Earth.

When we connect our bodies to the Earth, we are absorbing the Earth's energy. The Earth is full of electricity. Big, bold, powerful electricity! Did you know that your body is also full of electricity?

Plants, trees, water, air, animals, and insects are all part of nature. Humans are part of nature too. There are many amazing things that humans have that other parts of nature do not. Things such as living in houses, riding in cars, wearing shoes, playing on turf or concrete, and playing video games makes life comfortable, but these things also limit our contact with the Earth's surface.

The Earth is electric and full of limitless electrons. These electrons are invisible to the human eye. Our bodies need this electricity from the Earth, but we can only receive it when we are physically connected to the Earth's surface.

When our bodies are sick, tired, or have stress from worrying too much, our bodies create free radicals. We don't like free radicals. Free radicals are not good for us. When we connect our bodies directly to the Earth, our bodies absorb these electrons. These electrons help fight off and reduce free radicals. This creates a balance in our body. Balance is good.

So when someone tells you to eat your vegetables for good nutrition, remind them that getting your vitamin G -for grounding- is a part of your electrical nutrition!

Always ask an adult before you take off your shoes to play outside and be sure to check the ground for anything that may hurt you. Watch out for sharp rocks, sticks, or other objects before you go barefoot. If you prefer to keep your shoes on, don't worry! You can still get the same benefits from sitting or laying on the ground. You can also try hugging a tree to receive energy.

P.S. Don't forget to take your favorite pets with you. Pets need to practice grounding too.

The big, round Earth,
the bright blue sky.

4

Miles and miles to explore.

Breathing

Moving

Changing

Living

From insects buried
in the sand,

to cottonseed and
apple trees, spread
across the land.

Water flowing, soft winds blowing.

Over the hills, across the ocean, the energy flows and is put into motion.

Take off your socks and wiggle your toes, the Earth is conducting and the energy grows.

The energy comes from under our feet.

14

When we live in a house, or put shoes on our soles, it blocks out the energy that flows from below.

Long, long ago, before sidewalks and gravel,

many years before we could fly or travel.

16

We lived in nature and were one with the Earth. We played all day running about.

Let's bring this fun back
and bring back the day,

when little toes traveled
every which way!

Big hills, little hills, no match for us.

Running and jumping,
we play until dusk.

There are so many things
your feet might feel.

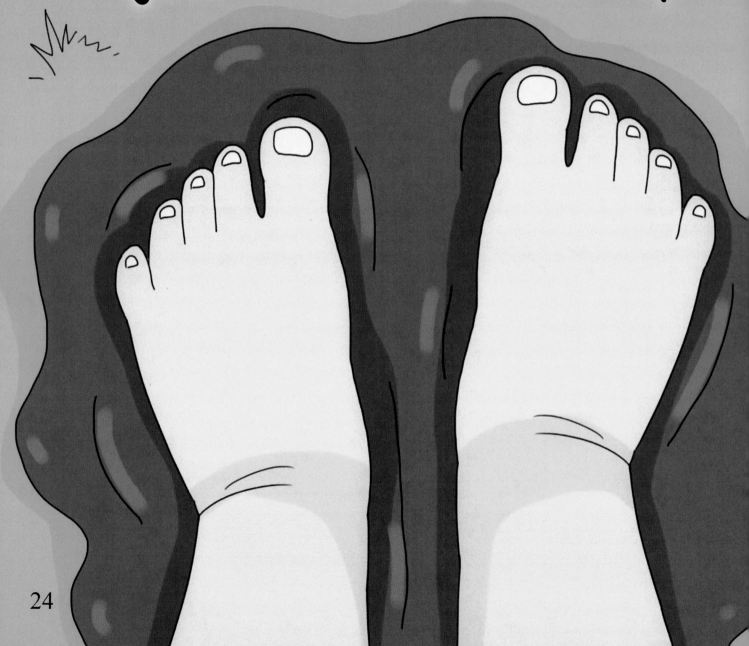

24

Be sure to check out our other titles for books on raising healthy and happy kids.

www.coachingwithdramandamorris.com

Made in the USA
Las Vegas, NV
09 August 2021